AIDAN DODSON

EGYPTIAN ROCK-CUT TOMBS

SHIRE EGYPTOLOGY

Cover illustration
The Middle Kingdom rock tombs of Beni Hasan
(from Lepsius, *Denkmäler*, Berlin/Leipzig, 1849-56).

British Library Cataloguing in Publication Data:
Dodson, Aidan.
Egyptian rock-cut tombs. — (Shire Egyptology, 14.)
I. Egypt. Rock tombs. Excavation of remains.
I. Title
932
ISBN 0-7478-0128-2

Published by
SHIRE PUBLICATIONS LTD
Cromwell House, Church Street, Princes Risborough,
Buckinghamshire HP17 9AJ, UK.

Series Editor: Barbara Adams.

Copyright © Aidan Dodson, 1991.

All rights reserved.
No part of this publication may be reproduced or transmitted
in any form or by any means, electronic or mechanical,
including photocopy, recording, or any information storage
and retrieval system, without permission in writing
from the publishers.

ISBN 0 7478 0128 2.

First published 1991.

Printed in Great Britain by
C. I. Thomas & Sons (Haverfordwest) Ltd,
Press Buildings, Merlins Bridge, Haverfordwest, Dyfed SA61 1XF.

Contents

LIST OF ILLUSTRATIONS 4

CHRONOLOGY 5

1. THE EGYPTIAN ROCK-CUT TOMB 7
2. THE OLD AND MIDDLE KINGDOMS 11
3. ROYAL TOMBS OF THE EIGHTEENTH DYNASTY 23
4. PRIVATE TOMBS OF THE NEW KINGDOM 33
5. ROYAL TOMBS OF THE RAMESSIDE ERA 43
6. LATER TOMBS 51
7. DESIGN AND CONSTRUCTION 56
8. THE FUTURE 61
9. FURTHER READING 62
10. MUSEUMS 63

INDEX 64

Acknowledgements

I must express my deepest gratitude to A. F. Shore and Pat Winker of the University of Liverpool for providing the photographs from their department's archives. Also to be thanked for photographs are the Petrie Museum of Egyptian Archaeology, University College London; and the Griffith Institute, University of Oxford. I am greatly indebted to David Rohl for his help with the preparation of many illustrations. Warmest thanks are due to Salima Ikram, Julie Hudson and Mark Collier for reading drafts of the text; its final form owes much to their comments. The dynastic chronology is based on that of Dr William J. Murnane and acknowledgement is made to him and to Penguin Books for its use here. Finally, I would like to thank my parents for their years of support: to them I dedicate this book.

Unless otherwise stated, the photographs and line drawings are by the author. (The arrows on the drawings indicate north.)

List of illustrations

1. Mortuary temple of Khaefre, Giza *page 8*
2. Ramesseum, Thebes *page 8*
3. Great Temple at Deir el-Bahri *page 9*
4. Rock tombs at Aswan *page 10*
5. Tomb of Seshemnefer IV, Giza *page 12*
6. Rock-cut tombs at Giza *page 12*
7. Interior of tomb at Kakherptah at Giza *page 13*
8. Private tomb chapels of the Old Kingdom *page 14*
9. Tombs south of causeway of Unas *page 15*
10. Tomb 18 at Beni Hasan *page 15*
11. Private tomb chapels of the Middle Kingdom *page 16*
12. Causeway leading to the tomb of Amenemhat *page 16*
13. Tomb of Amenemhat *page 17*
14. Tomb complex of Intef II at el-Tarif *page 18*
15. Corridor of the tomb of Mentuhotep III *page 18*
16. Burial chamber of Mentuhotep III *page 19*
17. Tomb of Meket-Re *page 19*
18. Burial chamber of Neterunakht and Khnumhotep *page 20*
19. (a) Royal cenotaph cemetery at Abydos; (b) substructure of 'tomb' of Sesostris III at Abydos *page 21*
20. Map of Western Thebes *page 22*
21. Entrance to the Kings' Valley *page 22*
22. Tombs of the kings of the earlier Eighteenth Dynasty *page 24*
23. Tombs of early Eighteenth Dynasty queens *page 25*
24. Isometric view of Eighteenth Dynasty royal burial chamber *page 26*
25. Antechamber of the tomb of Tuthmosis IV *page 26*
26. Chariot of Tuthmosis IV *page 27*
27. Tombs of the kings of the later Eighteenth Dynasty *page 28*
28. Decoration of burial chamber of Amenophis III *page 28*
29. Burial chamber and sarcophagus of Tutankhamun *page 29*
30. Antechamber of tomb of Horemheb *page 30*
31. Burial chamber of Horemheb *page 31*
32. Horemheb's crypt and sarcophagus *page 31*
33. Private tombs of Sheikh Abd el-Qurna *page 32*
34. Private tomb-chapels of the earlier Eighteenth Dynasty *page 32*
35. The tomb of Menena *page 34*
36. Sheikh Abd el-Qurna, with tomb of Ramose *page 35*
37. Private tomb-chapels of the reigns of Tuthmosis IV and Amenophis III *page 35*
38. (a) Forecourt of the tomb of Kheruef; (b) worship in the tombs of Userhat and Mahu *page 36*
39. Private tomb-chapels of late Eighteenth/early Nineteenth Dynasty *page 37*
40. (a) Interior of the tomb of Mahu; (b) tomb of Horemheb, Saqqara *pages 38-9*
41. New Kingdom tombs at Hierakonpolis *page 39*
42. Tomb of Nebwenenef: reconstruction and plan *page 40*
43. Private tomb-chapels of the Ramesside Period *page 41*
44. Necropolis of the workmen of the royal tomb, Deir el-Medina *page 44*

List of illustrations

45. Central area of the Kings' Valley *page 44*
46. Tombs of the kings of the Nineteenth Dynasty *page 45*
47. Burial chamber of Merneptah *page 46*
48. Left door jamb of the tomb of Amenmesse *page 47*
49. Tombs of the kings of the Twentieth Dynasty *page 47*
50. First corridor of the tomb of Ramesses VI *page 48*
51. Tombs of members of the Ramesside royal family *page 49*
52. Tomb of Mentuhirkopshef *page 50*
53. Tombs of the high priestesses at Medinet Habu *page 52*
54. Asasif, with Saite tombs *page 52*
55. Tomb of Pedamenopet *page 53*
56. Tombs at Tuna el-Gebel *page 54*
57. Tomb-chapel at Tuna el-Gebel *page 54*
58. Façade of tomb of Petosiris *page 55*
59. Tomb 11 at Beni Hasan *page 57*
60. Village of Deir el-Medina *page 58*
61. Workmen's huts on the col between Deir el-Medina and the Biban el-Moluk *page 59*
62. Map of Egypt *page 60*

Chronology

Early Dynastic or Archaic Period	3050 to 2613 BC		Dynasties I-II
Old Kingdom	2686 to 2181 BC		
		2686-2613	Dynasty III
		2613-2502	Dynasty IV
		2558-2528	*Khaefre*
		2525-2497	*Menkaure*
		2492-2181	Dynasties V-VI
First Intermediate Period	2181 to 2040 BC		
		2181-2040	Dynasties VII-X
		2160-2040	Dynasty XI(1)
		2123-2073	*Intef II*
Middle Kingdom	2040 to 1782 BC		
		2040-1994	Dynasty XI(2)
		(2065)-2014	*Mentuhotep II*
		2014-2001	*Mentuhotep III*
		1994-1782	Dynasty XII
		1932-1898	*Amenemhat II*
		1881-1842	*Sesostris III*
Second Intermediate Period	1782 to 1570 BC		
		1782-1650	Dynasty XIII
			Hor
		1710-1650	Dynasties XIV-XVI
		1650-1550	Dynasty XVII
		1560-1555	*Tao II*
		1555-1550	*Kamose*

New Kingdom	1550 to 1070 BC		
		1550-1293	Dynasty XVIII
		1550-1525	*Ahmose I*
		1525-1503	*Amenophis I*
		1503-1489	*Tuthmosis I*
		1489-1479	*Tuthmosis II*
		1479-1425	*Tuthmosis III*
		1472-1458	*Hatshepsut*
		1428-1397	*Amenophis II*
		1497-1386	*Tuthmosis IV*
		1386-1349	*Amenophis III*
		1350-1334	*Amenophis IV/Akhenaten*
		1336-1334	*Smenkhkare/Neferneferuaten*
		1334-1325	*Tutankhamun*
		1325-1321	*Ay*
		1321-1293	*Horemheb*
		1293-1185	Dynasty XIX
		1293-1291	*Ramesses I*
		1291-1278	*Seti I*
		1279-1212	*Ramesses II*
		1212-1200	*Merneptah*
		1200-1193	*Seti II*
		1198-1195	*Amenmesse*
		1193-1187	*Siptah*
		1187-1185	*Tawosret*
		1185-1070	Dynasty XX
		1185-1182	*Sethnakhte*
		1182-1151	*Ramesses III*
		1151-1145	*Ramesses IV*
		1145-1141	*Ramesses V*
		1141-1135	*Ramesses VI*
		1135-1129	*Ramesses VII*
		1129-1126	*Ramesses VIII*
		1126-1107	*Ramesses IX*
		1107-1097	*Ramesses X*
		1097-1070	*Ramesses XI*
Third Intermediate Period	1070 to 713 BC		
		1070-945	Dynasty XXI
		1040-991	*Psusennes I*
		979-960	*Siamun*
		945-718	Dynasty XXII
		874-850	*Osorkon II*
		870-860	*Harsiesis*
		818-713	Dynasties XXIII-XXIV
Late Period	713 to 332 BC		
		713-656	Dynasty XXV
		664-525	Dynasty XXVI
		525-332	Dynasties XXVII-XXXI
Graeco-Roman Period	332 BC to AD 395		
		332-330	Ptolemaic Dynasty
		310-282	*Ptolemy I*
		30 BC-AD 395	Roman Emperors

1
The Egyptian rock-cut tomb

In a sense, the vast majority of major Egyptian tombs were rock-cut; in spite of massive superstructures, almost all pyramids and mastabas (bench-shaped tombs) contained substructures cut in the rock, whether simple burial pits or elaborate labyrinths. However, for the purposes of this book, rock-cut tombs shall be defined as those designed and constructed without a significant built superstructure.

However they were constructed, Egyptian tombs were visualised as the eternal homes of the dead, to preserve the body and its effects intact, and to allow the spirit to obtain nourishment. To these ends, the ideal Egyptian tomb comprised two distinct elements: a subterranean burial chamber and, above the ground, an offering place or chapel. The former was sealed and inaccessible, but the chapel lay open, to receive those responsible for depositing offerings for the benefit of the spirit. That spirit would come forth to receive them, or to partake of 'the cool sweet breeze', through a 'false-door' stela or portrait statue that normally lay at the rear of the chapel (see figure 13).

Most private chapels were relatively modest, but those of kings usually took the form of fully fledged temples, adjoining the pyramid and burial chamber in the Old and Middle Kingdoms (figure 1), or some miles from an isolated subterranean sepulchral chamber in the New Kingdom (figures 2 and 3).

Among the nobility, the offering place lay either inside a built superstructure, during the Old and Middle Kingdoms of mastaba form, or within one or more chambers cut into the cliffs that line much of the length of the Egyptian Nile (figure 4), the choice normally depending on the configuration of the terrain.

In most non-royal cases the tomb chambers were cut into the rock below the chapel, often approached by a vertical shaft; however, in a number of instances their owners excavated their actual resting places some considerable distance away, a separation of tomb and chapel which had been initiated by the early kings of the New Kingdom.

If decorated at all, tomb chambers of both kings and commoners were usually adorned with mythological scenes and texts, particularly relating to the nocturnal voyage of the Sun God through the Underworld. While very few private burial chambers are decorated, most royal tombs of the New Kingdom and later carried such motifs, together with depictions of the king before the gods.

In contrast, the decoration of royal and private offering places differed substantially. The king was a god, and therefore his funerary chapel

1. Ruins of the mortuary temple of Khaefre, at the foot of the east face of his pyramid at Giza.

2. Part of the Ramesseum, the mortuary temple of Ramesses II at Thebes (Nineteenth Dynasty).

3. The Great Temple of Deir el-Bahri, the mortuary chapel of Hatshepsut (Eighteenth Dynasty).

was decorated in the manner of a temple of a deity, with scenes of the gods and their ceremonial. The decoration of the commoner's chapel, however, was concerned with his well-being in the agricultural afterlife of the 'Field of Reeds' and therefore centred on the so-called 'scenes of daily life', which tell us so much about life in ancient Egypt. While the simplest tombs had little more than a single false-door stela, many tombs contained extensive paintings and reliefs of almost every aspect of the life that the dead person wished to perpetuate in what the Egyptians termed 'The West' (*imntt*). Alongside their apparently simple evocation of life on earth, it has been argued that these scenes also have ritual significance, as examples of the multiplicity of meaning that can be seen in so many Egyptian contexts.

It seems that the ideal was for these scenes to be executed in painted relief, particularly when the chapel was built of, lined with or cut into good-quality stone, which was the case at the majority of sites; otherwise, flat colour was used, particularly at Thebes, where rock of a good enough quality for carving lies at a relatively low level. This could lead to a choice between a prominent position, high in the cliff face, with a painted decoration, and a less conspicuous location, but with the possibility of fine relief.

4. Old and Middle Kingdom rock tombs at Qubbet el-Hawa, Aswan.

Having now briefly outlined the basic considerations that lay behind the design and decoration of Egyptian tombs in general, and rock-cut ones in particular, the succeeding chapters will trace the latter's architectural development, highlighting some of the more significant innovations, concluding with a brief account of the practicalities of their construction, and the men responsible for it.

2
The Old and Middle Kingdoms

The very earliest Egyptian tombs were merely holes in the desert sand or gravel; however, from the dawn of history, progressive development introduced the lined and covered pit, the staircase entrance, the shaft entrance and the tunnelled substructure to the tombs of the rich. Most of these early tombs had some kind of superstructure, whether a simple mound or a properly built mastaba of brick or stone.

During the Early Dynastic Period modest offering places came to be built into superstructures, later expanding into larger cult complexes, which in some cases took up much of their volume (figure 5). In areas less suited to mastaba building these offering places came to be cut into cliff faces, overlooking the cultivated land bordering the Nile. Early major groups lie in former quarries at Giza (figure 6), others at the edge of the escarpment west of the Great Pyramid (figure 7); somewhat later are the tombs that are cut in the rock face just south of the causeway of the pyramid of Unas at Saqqara (figure 9).

Initially these chapels closely followed the design of those of contemporary mastabas but, as the Old Kingdom progressed, distinctive rock-cut forms began to be developed (figure 8). At the same time the number of major tombs built away from the Memphite necropolis grew considerably, the cliffs of Middle and Upper Egypt providing ideal sites for rock tombs (see figure 4), contrasting with the relatively flat areas that characterise much of Saqqara and Giza.

By the end of the Sixth Dynasty rock-cut tomb chapels were becoming quite elaborate, a trend that continued during the First Intermediate Period, a time of little centralised control during which local governors, or nomarchs, achieved high levels of power. Large rock-cut cemeteries had now arisen, in which provincial grandees were laid to rest surrounded by the pit tombs of their retainers; an example of such a necropolis is provided by the Middle Egyptian site of Beni Hasan, where a series of nomarchs' tombs runs from the latter part of the First Intermediate Period down to the time of Sesostris III of the Twelfth Dynasty. Here one may see the progressive elaboration of chapel plans, from a simple square room, devoid of pillars, to a pillared hall, fronted by a columned portico (figures 10, 11, 12, 13 and front cover).

The building of the earlier of the Beni Hasan tombs approximately coincided with the opening of hostilities between the two territorial groupings that had coalesced out of Egypt's disunity towards the end of the First Intermediate Period. This drawn-out struggle culminated in the re-establishment of central control under King Mentuhotep II of

5. Portico of the mastaba chapel of Seshemnefer IV at Giza (LG 53 - Fifth/Sixth Dynasty); to the right are the pyramids of two wives of Khufu.

6. Fourth-Fifth Dynasty rock-cut tombs at Giza, south-west of the Second Pyramid.

The Old and Middle Kingdoms

Thebes, c.2040 BC, thus beginning the Middle Kingdom.

The earliest rock tomb chapels belonging to this city lie on a low hill at Thebes, now known as Khokha (see figure 20), and date to the very end of the Old Kingdom, but the Intefs, the nomarchs who assumed royal titles at Thebes c.2140 BC, chose a site for their tombs further

7. (right and below). Two views of the interior of the tomb-chapel of Kakherptah at Giza (Fifth Dynasty).

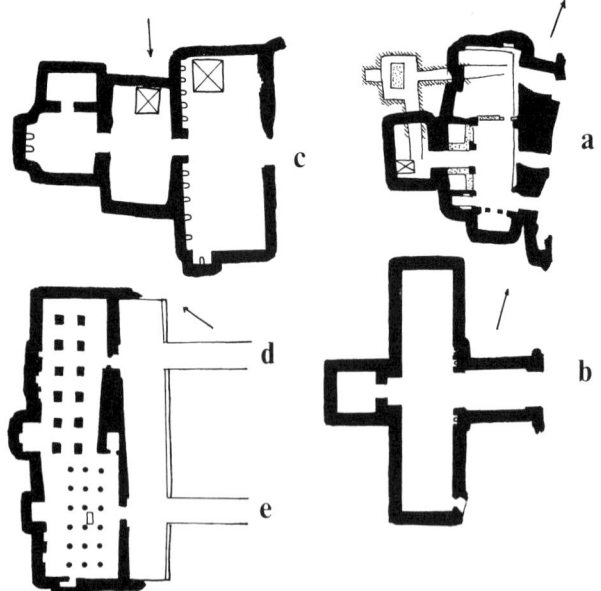

8. Private tomb-chapels of the Old Kingdom. (a) Debhen (time of Menkaure — Giza LG 90); (b) Khenuka (Fifth Dynasty — Tihna 14); (c) Meru-Bebi (Sixth Dynasty — Sheikh Said 3); (d) Sabni; (e) Mekhu (Sixth Dynasty — Aswan 26 and 25).

north, at el-Tarif, an area that had seen use during the Old Kingdom, including the erection of two large mastabas. Here, in the gravel plain, large courtyards were sunk, at the back of which a colonnade gave access to the chapels and tomb-shafts of the kinglets; other entrances gave access to the tombs of the court (figure 14). These tombs are now known as *saff*, the Arabic for 'row', and, contrary to earlier Egyptological opinion, do not appear to have been surmounted by pyramids.

Mentuhotep II of the Eleventh Dynasty forsook el-Tarif for the valley of Deir el-Bahri, some way to the south; here he built his terraced temple, behind which a long rock-cut gallery gave access to the sepulchral chamber. This contained an alabaster shrine within which the king was laid to rest. His successor, Mentuhotep III, began a similar monument further south, which remained unfinished (figures 15 and 16).

Members of the Mentuhoteps' courts made their tombs nearby, most of which comprised a flat façade giving access to a long decorated corridor, at the end of which a shaft or passageway gave access to the burial. The façade was often fronted by a sloping courtyard and, in some cases, incorporated a colonnade (figure 11, a).

The funerary equipment of all these tombs was distinctive, including, besides the coffin, a whole series of wooden models of various aspects of daily life. Although examples were found in the tomb of Mentuhotep

The Old and Middle Kingdoms

9. Old Kingdom tombs south of the causeway of Unas, Saqqara.

10. Pillared hall of unfinished tomb chapel 18 at Beni Hasan, Eleventh Dynasty. (Courtesy of the School of Archaeology and Oriental Studies, University of Liverpool.)

Egyptian Rock-cut Tombs

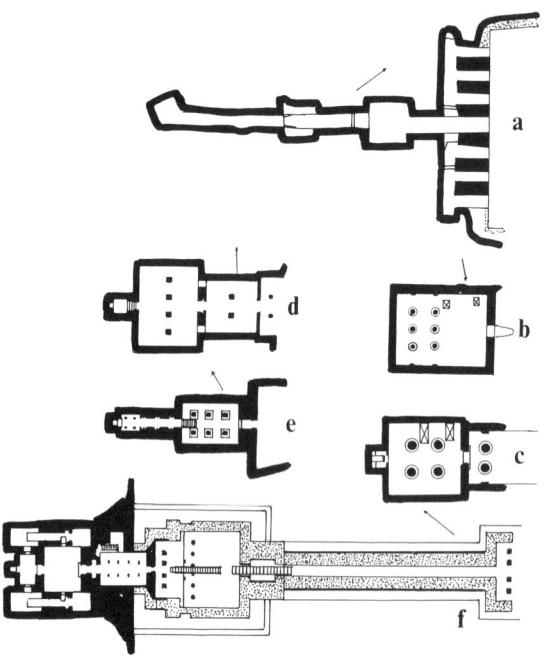

11. (Left) Private tomb-chapels of the Middle Kingdom. (a) Dagi (Eleventh Dynasty — TT103, Sheikh Abd el-Qurna); (b) Khety (Eleventh Dynasty — Beni Hasan 17); (c) Amenemhat (time of Sesostris I — Beni Hasan 2); (d) Nekht Ankh (Twelfth Dynasty — Deir Rifeh); (e) Sarenput II (time of Amenemhat II — Aswan 31); (f) Wahka I (Twelfth Dynasty — Qau el-Kebir).

12. (Below) Beni Hasan: the causeway leading up to the tomb of Amenemhat. (Courtesy of the School of Archaeology and Oriental Studies, University of Liverpool.)

The Old and Middle Kingdoms

II himself, the finest come from the tomb of Meket-Re, chancellor of Mentuhotep III (figure 17). Many other sets of models have come to light in tombs of the period, particularly well known being those from the shaft tombs at Beni Hasan.

13. Tomb of Amenemhat at Beni Hasan, with destroyed cult statue at rear. (Courtesy of the School of Archaeology and Oriental Studies, University of Liverpool.)

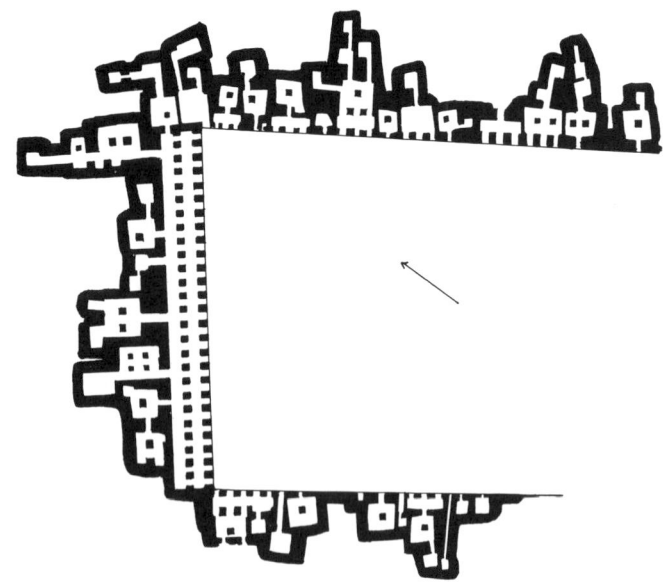

14. Tomb complex of Intef II at el-Tarif (Saff el-Kisasiya).

15. Entrance corridor of the tomb of Mentuhotep III, TT 281, behind Sheikh Abd el-Qurna.

The Old and Middle Kingdoms

16. Angled limestone roofing blocks of the burial chamber of Mentuhotep III.

Following the demise of Mentuhotep IV, who has no known tomb, the kings of the next dynasty, the Twelfth, re-established the royal seat of power in the north and moved their cemeteries to the area of Memphis and the Fayum. There they built tombs of classic pyramidal form and, by virtue of the topographies of these sites, the private tombs constructed there were largely of mastaba shape.

17. Tomb of Meket-Re, TT 280, behind Sheikh Abd el-Qurna, time of Mentuhotep III.

In Middle and Upper Egypt the private tombs of the Middle Kingdom continued the tradition of being cut high in the cliffs flanking the river. The decoration was finely carved at, for example, Meir and Asyut, and painted at sites such as Beni Hasan. The architecture of some tombs became particularly complex, three examples at Qau el-Kebir being joined to the riverbank by causeways and courtyards of stone and brick (figure 11, f). The series of great provincial private tombs seems to die out in the latter part of the Twelfth Dynasty; the cessation of their construction has been explained as being the result of a conscious royal act to reduce the power of the local rulers, but the evidence is by no means decisive.

While the kings of the Twelfth Dynasty were all buried under pyramids, Sesostris III also possessed a purely rock-cut tomb, which formed part of a cenotaph at Abydos, holy city of Osiris, King of the Dead (figure 19). Although the king was buried at Dahshur, the 'tomb' was equipped with a granite sarcophagus and canopic chest and was elabo-

18. Burial chamber of the pit tomb of Neterunakht, Khnumhotep and others at Beni Hasan (294), viewed from the bottom of the shaft. (Courtesy of the School of Archaeology and Oriental Studies, University of Liverpool.)

The Old and Middle Kingdoms

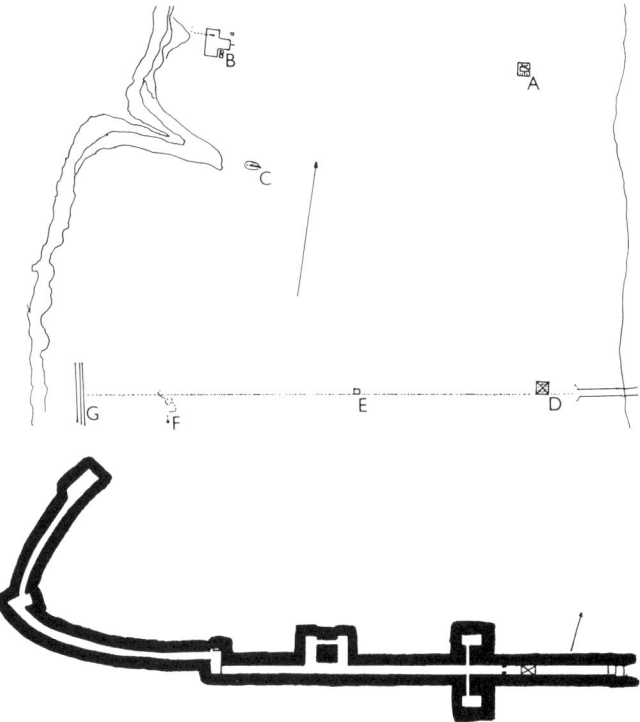

19. (Top) Royal cenotaph cemetery at Abydos: A, chapel of Sesostris III; B, 'tomb' of Sesostris III; C, unfinished tomb; D, pyramid of Ahmose I; E, chapel of Tetisheri, mother of Ahmose I; F, 'tomb' of Ahmose I; G, temple of Ahmose I. (Bottom) Substructure of 'tomb' of Sesostris III at Abydos.

rately protected with plug blocks and dummy passages: none of these, however, prevented its pillage in antiquity.

With the advent of the Thirteenth Dynasty the realm once again began to move on a downward path, the country eventually splitting, with the north under the control of the Palestinian Hyksos rulers. Only a handful of persons are known to have built monumental tombs during this period, most being satisfied with modest pit graves. Such individuals included kings: Hor, a ruler of the Thirteenth Dynasty, was buried in a shaft at Dahshur that had originally been intended for a follower of Amenemhat III. Modified to make its burial chamber resemble that of a contemporary pyramid, with a pointed roof and close-fitting sarcophagus and canopic chest, it was still partly intact when entered in 1894 and gives us our earliest glimpse of the contents of a king's tomb, including a gilded mask over the mummy's head and fine wooden statues.

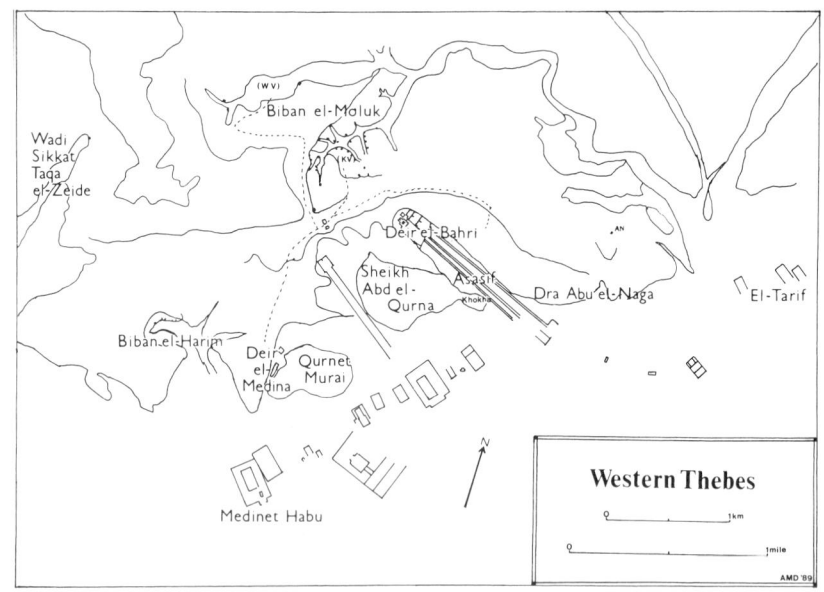

20. Map of Western Thebes.

21. Entrance to the Kings' Valley, showing the pyramidal peak of el-Qurn. (From Lepsius, *Denkmäler*, Berlin/Leipzig, 1849-56, I, plate 95.)

3
Royal tombs of the Eighteenth Dynasty

The earlier reigns

As had been the case at the end of the First Intermediate Period, Egypt's unity was restored through the efforts of the princes of Thebes after the disintegration of the Second Intermediate Period. Most prominent among them were the last two rulers of the Seventeenth Dynasty, Tao II and Kamose, together with their kinsman and successor Ahmose I, founder of the Eighteenth Dynasty. The early members of this royal house had founded a line of small pyramids along the front of Dra Abu el-Naga, the latest known, from written records, being that of Kamose.

It is unclear where the tomb of Ahmose was situated; some have argued that it lay near those of his immediate ancestors, but it is possible that he was the first king to construct a tomb in a wadi that lies behind the curtain of cliffs that are a distinctive feature of the Theban necropolis, a place now known to the world as the Valley of the Kings (Biban el-Moluk) (figures 20 and 21). If he did so, he will have been the first to take the momentous step of separating the burial chamber from the funerary chapel; hitherto, these structures had been placed close together to allow the spirit easy access to its offerings, but during the New Kingdom kings, and some of their subjects, began to place them far apart, convenience being subordinated to security from the ubiquitous tomb robber.

Like Sesostris III of the Middle Kingdom before him, Ahmose I possessed a cenotaph at Abydos (figure 19), the subterranean element of which comprised a winding passage interrupted by a pillared hall (figure 22, a). The latter has now collapsed and nothing survived of the cenotaph's contents save a few fragments of gold leaf.

The offering chapel of Ahmose remains unknown but that of his son, Amenophis I, seems to have lain at Deir el-Bahri, just north of the temple-tomb of Mentuhotep II. His tomb has likewise been the subject of debate but may be that which lies at the very southern end of the eastern branch (Kings' Valley) of the Biban el-Moluk (KV 39 in the catalogue of the valley's sepulchres). Excavations begun in 1989 have shown the tomb to be of most unusual form, probably the result of later extensions.

Uncertainty also exists over the tombs intended for the next two kings, Tuthmosis I and II; the balance of probability points to KV 20 and 42 being those originally cut for each of them. The former (figure 22, b) is simply a burial chamber approached by three long corridors, but KV 42 (figure 22, c) introduces three distinctive features. The first

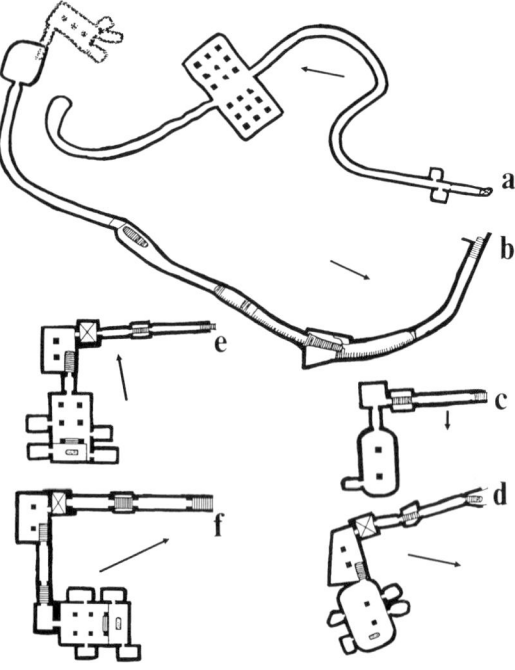

22. Tombs of the kings of the earlier Eighteenth Dynasty: (a) Ahmose I (Abydos cenotaph); (b) Tuthmosis I and Hatshepsut (Biban el-Moluk, KV 20); (c) Tuthmosis II (KV 42); (d) Tuthmosis III (KV 34); (e) Amenophis II (KV 35); (f) Tuthmosis IV (KV 43).

is a bent axis, typical of royal tombs over the next 130 years; the second is an oval burial chamber, apparently imitating the cartouche, the frame which surrounds each of two principal names of the kings of Egypt. The third is the reintroduction of the stone sarcophagus after a considerable hiatus: the last definite example had been used back in the Thirteenth Dynasty. All subsequent kings' tombs had one, until new arrangements appeared briefly towards the end of the Twentieth Dynasty.

The tombs of the first two queens of the dynasty, Ahmose-Nefertari and Meryetamun, respectively lay on top of Dra Abu el-Naga and at Deir el-Bahri, where Amenophis I had his mortuary chapel. Tuthmosis II's wife, Hatshepsut, cut hers in a wadi considerably further south; while acting as regent for her stepson, Tuthmosis III, she added a sarcophagus reminiscent of that of her late husband (figure 23).

After seven years as regent, Hatshepsut succeeded in obtaining pharaonic titles as co-ruler with Tuthmosis III; as such she built a now celebrated funerary temple at Deir-el-Bahri (figure 3) and seems to have extended the tomb of her father, adding a pillared burial chamber and preparing a joint burial in it within two quartzite sarcophagi.

The walls of this chamber were to have been lined with limestone

Royal tombs of the Eighteenth Dynasty

23. Tombs of early Eighteenth Dynasty queens: (a) Ahmose-Nefertari (Dra Abu el-Naga); (b) Meryetamun (TT 358, Deir el-Bahri); (c) Hatshepsut (Wadi Sikkat Taqa el-Zeide).

blocks, painted with the Book of Amduat ('What is in the Underworld'); little survives, but a full example of the intended scheme of decoration is to be found in the cartouche-shaped burial chamber of KV 34, the tomb of Tuthmosis III (figure 22, d). The walls of this room are adorned with a cursive version of the Book, rapidly sketched on a yellowish background, giving the impression that the walls are covered with an immense sheet of papyrus (see figure 28). The walls of KV 42 appear to have been prepared for such texts but were never finished.

A third cartouche-form chamber was decorated in the same manner, that of KV 38, a small tomb which seems to have been cut by Tuthmosis III to take the mummy of Tuthmosis I after removing it from KV 20: in the latter part of his reign the younger king had undertaken the desecration and dismantling of Hatshepsut's monuments.

Tuthmosis III's tomb is the prototype for subsequent kingly tombs of the New Kingdom, in particular introducing a deep 'well' into the plan, found earlier in the tombs of Queens Ahmose-Nefertari and Meryetamun. This seems to have had two roles, ritual and practical, the latter being the protection of the tomb from flooding, the former providing access to the subterranean and aquatic regions of the earth. Another element found in subsequent tombs is the pillared antechamber directly following the well; in KV 34 this contained a particularly extensive list of deities.

Tuthmosis' mortuary temple lay in front of Sheikh Abd el-Qurna and, like those of Hatshepsut and a number of others going back to the Middle Kingdom, was built in terraces. It is now very badly ruined, as are nearly all of the royal mortuary temples of the New Kingdom, little more than the ground plans surviving of most of the line that stretched from Qurna (Seti I) in the north to Medinet Habu (Ramesses III) in the south. In general, these sanctuaries conform to the plan of contemporary temples dedicated to major deities, with the addition of an extra court, dedicated to the sun.

The temple of Amenophis II, son of Tuthmosis III, is almost totally destroyed, but his tomb survives in excellent condition. It closely follows the design of that of his father, with the exception of a more regular plan

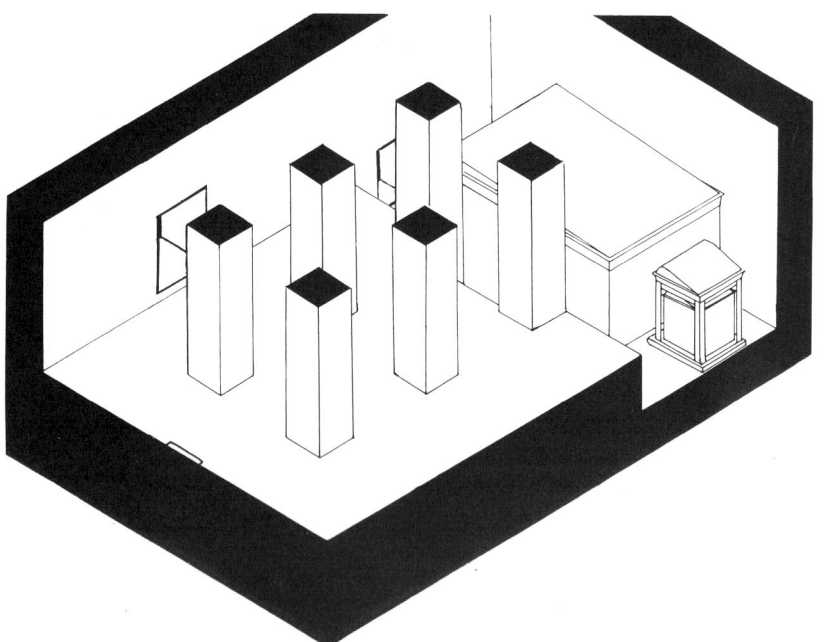

24. Isometric view of a mid/late Eighteenth Dynasty king's burial chamber, showing the crypt, with its enshrined sarcophagus and canopic chest.

25. East wall of the antechamber of the tomb of Tuthmosis IV. (Courtesy of the School of Archaeology and Oriental Studies, University of Liverpool.)

Royal tombs of the Eighteenth Dynasty

26. Chariot body of Tuthmosis IV as discovered in the burial chamber of his tomb. (Courtesy of the School of Archaeology and Oriental studies, University of Liverpool.)

and, perhaps surprisingly, the abandonment of the cartouche-form burial chamber in favour of a columned, rectangular apartment, with a sunken crypt at its far end (figure 22, e). This feature seems to have been introduced to provide adequate clearance for the installation of a nest of shrines around the sarcophagus, examples of which were found in the tomb of Tutankhamun (figure 24). The decoration of the chamber walls follows that found in KV 34, but the pillars bear detailed representations of the king before various deities.

The tombs of Tuthmosis IV (KV 43) and Amenophis III (WV 22) are essentially expansions of KV 35 (figures 22, f, and 27, a), with a progressive increase in the number of scenes of the king with the gods, which now spill over into the antechamber and well-room (figure 25).

The Amarna Period and its aftermath

This steady development of royal tombs was interrupted by the 'religious revolution' of Akhenaten, involving the replacement of the age-old pantheon with the worship of the single Sun God, the Aten, and the king's removal to a new capital at Tell el-Amarna in Middle Egypt. There he cut his tomb (figure 27, b), presumably replacing one begun at Thebes at the outset of his reign. Although never finished, it differs from preceding tombs in both decoration and design. The most remarkable aspects of the latter are the suites of rooms cut off from the main corridor, one of which takes the form of a complete royal tomb in itself, perhaps intended for Queen Nefertiti. The other set (the cutting of

Egyptian Rock-cut Tombs

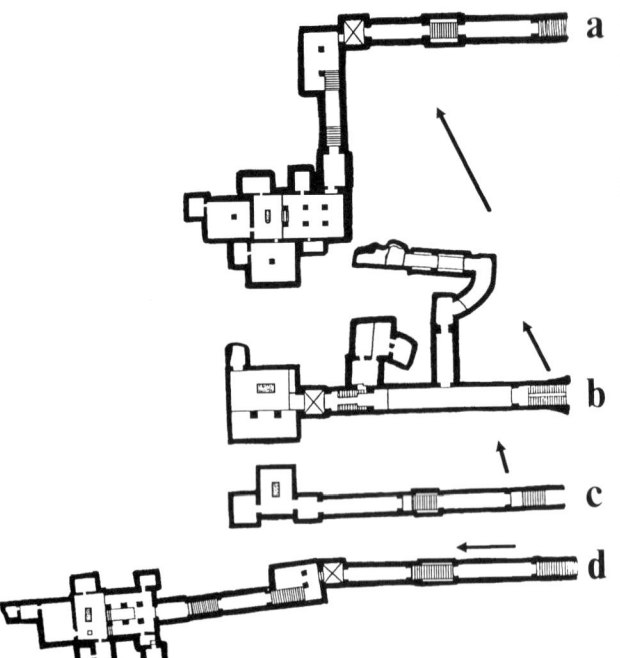

27. (Left) Tombs of the kings of the later Eighteenth Dynasty: (a) Amenophis III (Biban el-Moluk, WV 22); (b) Akhenaten (Wadi Abu Hasah el-Bahri, Tell el-Amarna 26); (c) Ay (WV 23); (d) Horemheb (KV 57).

28. (Below) Detail of the decoration of the burial chamber of the tomb of Amenophis III, drawn in pen on yellow ground in imitation of a funerary papyrus. (From Lepsius, *Denkmäler*, Berlin/Leipzig, 1849-56, III, plate 79.)

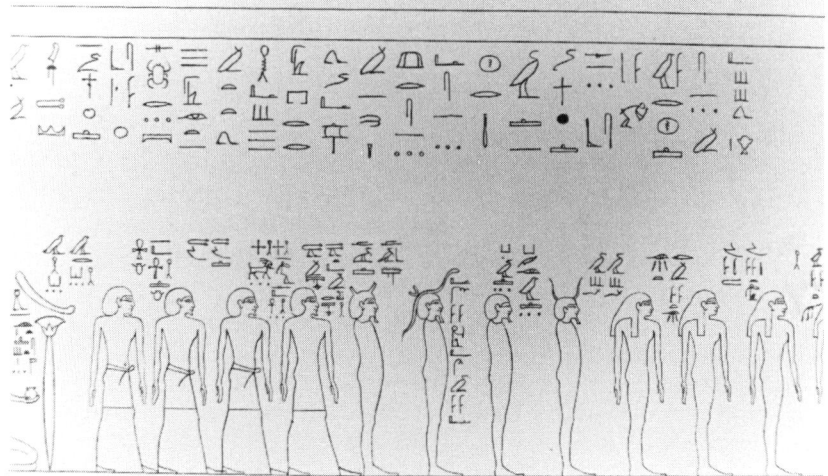

Royal tombs of the Eighteenth Dynasty

29. Burial chamber and sarcophagus of Tutankhamun. (Harry Burton, courtesy of the Griffith Institute, Oxford.)

others had barely begun) had contained the burials of the Princess Meketaten and another lady, perhaps his second wife, Kiya. In their decoration, the chambers no longer bore the Amduat and its denizens of the underworld; in their place were scenes of the worship of the Aten (see figure 38, b) and the mourning of the deceased. In execution, too, the depictions differed from the previous royal norm, being carved in

30. Antechamber of the tomb of Horemheb, showing dumped chips from the tomb's construction. (From Davis *et.al.*, *The Tombs of Harmhabi and Touatânkhamanou*, London, 1912, plate XLII.)

relief rather than executed in flat line and/or colour; this feature was to be adopted for most later royal tombs.

Akhenaten's successors, Smenkhkhare/Neferneferuaten and Tutankhaten/amun, may have begun one or more of the unfinished tombs which lie near Akhenaten's, but Tutankhamun soon abandoned Amarna and probably began work on a tomb in the West Valley of the Biban el-Moluk, where Amenophis III had been buried. However, he was actually buried in a hastily enlarged private sepulchre in the Kings' Valley, now numbered KV 62. Only one room was ever decorated, including, alongside extracts from the Amduat, scenes of a kind more usually found in private tomb-chapels: the dragging of the mummy to the tomb and the ceremony of Opening the Mouth, by means of which the corpse regained the ability to take sustenance.

By a stroke of fate, KV 62 was to remain essentially intact until 1922, giving us our first, and only, example of the full burial outfit of a king of Egypt at the height of the country's wealth and power. Pitiful fragments from other tombs help us reconstruct how such an assemblage would have lain in a full-size king's tomb: a royal sarcophagus was enclosed within a series of gilded shrines and lay in the crypt of its burial hall, surrounded by the enshrined figures of deities, with the canopic chest, containing the embalmed internal organs, at its foot (figure 24). The pillared part of the chamber contained many further items

Royal tombs of the Eighteenth Dynasty

of equipment, including pieces of furniture and chariots, with the crypt guarded by large wooden statues of the king. Further material was stored in the four annexes that generally open out of the hall. Large pottery jars containing provisions, including grain and water, were placed in the room at the foot of the sarcophagus, meat in the room at the body's head, just as foodstuffs had been since far-off Predynastic and Archaic times. The other annexes seem to have been intended respectively for faience vases and shabtis, the magical servants of the dead.

Tutankhamun's putative West Valley tomb (WV 23: figure 27, c) was occupied by his elderly successor, Ay, who decorated it with a similarly unusual selection of paintings. His burial seems, however, to have been perfunctory at the best and was later desecrated.

The last king of the dynasty was Horemheb, a soldier who had held high office under his immediate predecessors. He was buried in KV 57, a large tomb best viewed as being of the same form as Amenhotep III's with its axis straightened out (figure 27, d). The tomb is important as the first in the Biban el-Moluk to have carved decoration (figure 30), unfinished in the burial chamber (figures 31 and 32).

31. Collapsed pillar in the burial chamber of Horemheb. (From Davis *et.al.*, *The Tombs of Harmhabi and Touatânkhamanou*, London, 1912, plate XLVI.)

32. Horemheb's crypt and sarcophagus: his was the last of the four sarcophagi of the late Eighteenth Dynasty that placed divine female figures at the corners. (From Davis *et al.*, *The Tombs of Harmhabi and Touatânkhamanou*, London, 1912, plate LXVI.

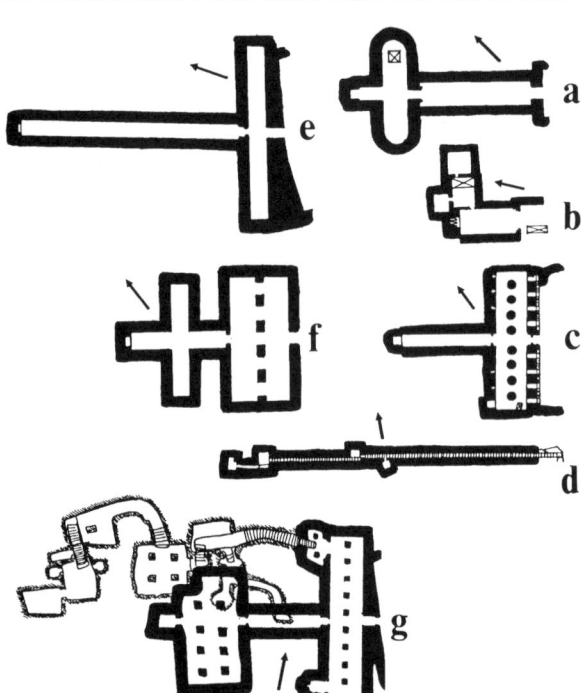

33. Private tombs of Sheikh Abd el-Qurna. (From Lepsius, *Denkmäler*, Berlin/Leipzig, 1849-56, I, plate 67.)

34. Private tomb-chapels of the earlier Eighteenth Dynasty: (a) Ken (early Eighteenth Dynasty — TT 59, Sheikh Abd el-Qurna); (b) Paheri (early Tuthmosis III — el-Kab 3); (c) Senenmut (time of Hatshepsut — TT 71, Sheikh Abd el-Qurna); (d) Senenmut — tomb chambers (TT 353, Deir el-Bahri); (e) Rekhmire (TT 100); (f) Amenemheb (TT 85 — both Sheikh Abd el-Qurna, time of Tuthmosis III-Amenophis II); (g) Kenamun (time of Amenophis II — TT 93, Sheikh Abd el-Qurna).

4
Private tombs of the New Kingdom

The earlier Eighteenth Dynasty at Thebes

The victory of the Theban kings over the Hyksos was marked by a revival of the cutting of major tombs in the city's necropolis (figure 20). Some of the earlier tombs may have been usurpations of Middle Kingdom examples, but at an early stage a basic form became established that was to be the basis of the majority of tomb-chapel plans at Thebes and other sites.

This form, perhaps derived from the porticoed tombs of the Middle Kingdom (compare figure 11, a), is best described as an inverted T: from a forecourt, a doorway leads to a chamber running parallel to, and just behind, the face of the cliff; directly opposite the entrance, a passageway leads back into the rock, with the principal offering place at its end. There are many variations and elaborations on the theme, some tombs being additionally surmounted by a small pyramid (compare figures 42 and 44).

Although no two tombs are alike, many chapels have a similar layout of painted scenes upon their walls: offering scenes either side of the entrance, such 'daily life' depictions as hunting, winemaking and agriculture in the front chamber, with the funerary procession, rites before the corpse and the symbolic voyage to Abydos, the sacred city of Osiris, King of the Dead, in the rear passage.

Burial chambers normally lie deep in the rock below the chapel, approached in most cases by a shaft, but in some cases by an inclined or stepped passageway.

The earliest tombs of the Eighteenth Dynasty lie on Dra Abu el-Naga, but later ones were built further south at Sheikh Abd el-Qurna, where lie many of the finest tombs in the necropolis. One of the first chapels to be excavated there was that of Senenmut (figure 34, c), favourite of Queen Hatshepsut; the burial chamber lay, however, at the end of a long passage at Deir el-Bahri, within the precincts of his royal mistress's temple (figure 34, d). Curiously, the smashed fragments of his stone sarcophagus, a rare item for a commoner, were found in his chapel, rather than the burial chamber.

During the reigns of Tuthmosis III and Amenophis II, more elaborate tomb plans began to appear alongside the dominant 'T'; as well as the addition of columns and further rooms to the chapel, some tombs gained elaborate substructures including pillared halls. A good example at this date is the tomb of Kenamun (figure 34, g), also interesting for the unusual yellow background upon which the chapel's paintings are executed.

The provinces

While large numbers of tombs lie at Thebes, cemeteries with sepulchres dating to the first half of the Eighteenth Dynasty are known throughout Egypt, although in many cases poorly recorded. Tombs worthy of note are to be found at such sites as Edfu, el-Kab, Rifeh and Hierakonpolis (figure 41). Some of the best known are at el-Kab, particularly those of Paheri (figure 34, b), Ahmose-Pennekhbet (EK 2) and Ahmose son of Ibana (EK 5), the latter two containing important texts relating to the liberation of Egypt from the Hyksos.

Of somewhat later date are three tombs at Aniba and Toshka, in the Egyptian colonial province of Nubia: although of classic Egyptian form and decoration, their owners were native princes, publicly absorbed into the culture of their overlords.

35. Left-hand end of the cross-hall of the tomb of Menena (TT 69): the owner and his wife, Henttawi, adoring Osiris. (Siegfried Schott, courtesy of the Griffith Institute, Oxford.)

36. Old view of the Sheikh Abd el-Qurna hill, with the tomb of Ramose (TT 55) in the foreground. (Courtesy of the School of Archaeology and Oriental Studies, University of Liverpool.)

The reigns of Tuthmosis IV and Amenophis III

During the short reign of Tuthmosis IV and the long tenure of Amenophis III some of the finest tombs in the Theban necropolis were constructed, both simple painted chapels and some extremely elaborate carved tombs. The latter are generally cut low down in the Sheikh Abd el-Qurna/Khokha area, where the rock is of sufficiently good quality to

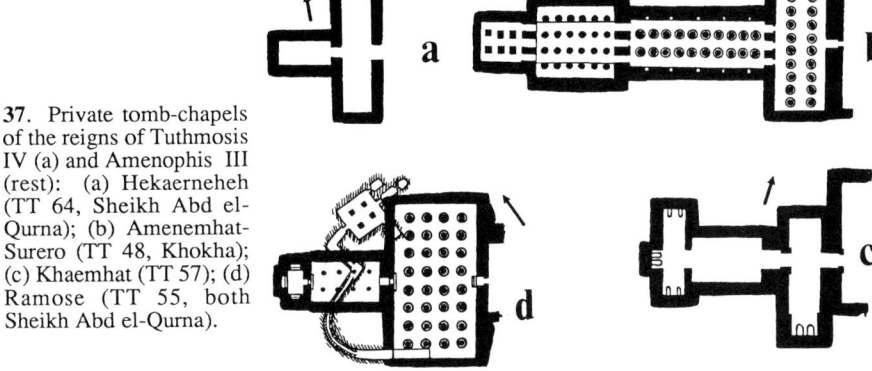

37. Private tomb-chapels of the reigns of Tuthmosis IV (a) and Amenophis III (rest): (a) Hekaerneheh (TT 64, Sheikh Abd el-Qurna); (b) Amenemhat-Surero (TT 48, Khokha); (c) Khaemhat (TT 57); (d) Ramose (TT 55, both Sheikh Abd el-Qurna).

38. (a: above) Forecourt of the tomb of Kheruef (TT 192): Khokha, time of Amenophis III/IV. (b: below) Worship of the sun: traditional versus Amarna. Left, Userhat pays homage to Re-Harakhty in the form of a hawk (time of Seti I — TT 51, Sheikh Abd el-Qurna); right, Akhenaten and Nefertiti offer to Aten, in the form of a rayed globe (tomb of Mahu, TA 9, Tell el-Amarna). (Courtesy of Petrie Museum of Egyptian Archaeology.)

Private tombs of the New Kingdom

support relief; higher up, carving is almost impossible. Amongst these low-cut tombs is that of the vizier Ramose (figures 36 and 37, d), with decoration in three styles: the superb low relief of Amenophis III's reign, the 'revolutionary' carved art of Amenophis IV (Akhenaten), and a fine funeral procession, painted on a flat ground at the noble's premature death.

Slightly earlier are the chapel of Khaemhat (figure 37, c), renowned for its relief work, and the gigantic monument of the chief steward, Amenemhat-Surero, now badly damaged, but the largest example of its genre, with a floor area of approximately 600 square metres (figure 37, b). Another huge tomb is that of Kheruef, finely decorated with scenes including both Amenophis III and IV in traditional style, but largely collapsed (figure 38, a).

The Amarna Period

A number of tombs at Thebes contain scenes in the new art style of Amarna, but the majority of private tombs thus far known from the reign of Akhenaten lie at the short-lived city of Akhetaten (Tell el-Amarna). At least one man, Parennefer, decorated a chapel at both sites. In design Amarna tombs largely follow plans used at Thebes in the immediately preceding period (figures 39, a, b, and 40, a) but in decoration they differ entirely. In place of the 'daily life' scenes, we find reliefs dealing with the life of the royal family, at home, in the city and in the temple (figure 38, b); but rarely is a figure of the tomb owner seen. Although he is usually shown at prayer, other representations tend to be limited to scenes of his reward by the king, and perhaps an appearance as a subsidiary figure in others.

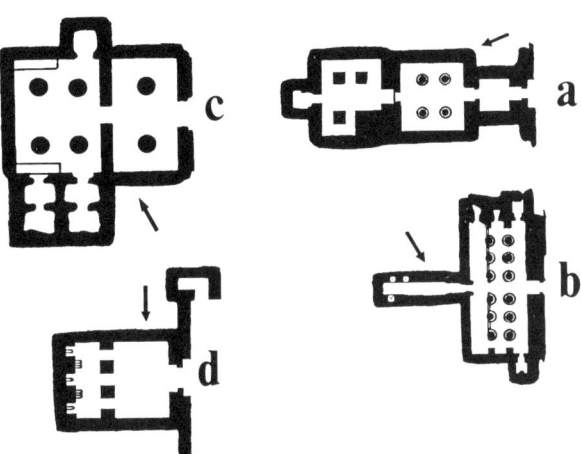

39. Private tomb-chapels of late Eighteenth/early Nineteenth Dynasty: (a) Meryre I (TA 4); (b) Tutu (TA 8, both Tell el-Amarna, time of Akhenaten); (c) Amenhotep (Qarat Hilwah, Bahriya Oasis); (d) Nefersekheru (Zawiyet el-Maiytin — Kom el-Ahmar).

40. (a) Interior of the rock-cut tomb-chapel of Mahu at Tell el-Amarna (TA 9, time of Akhenaten). (Courtesy of the Petrie Museum of Egyptian Archaeology.) (For figure 40, b, see facing page, top.)

40. (b) Free-standing chapel of Horemheb at Saqqara, time of Tutankhamun/Ay, partly restored. (For figure 40, a, see facing page.)

Few, if any, of the two dozen chapels were ever completed or show signs of use for burials; while most of their owners' fates are unknown, one, Ay, survived to become king on the death of Tutankhamun.

41. New Kingdom tomb-chapels on the Berg el-Hamman at Hierakonpolis. (Courtesy of the School of Archaeology and Oriental Studies, University of Liverpool.)

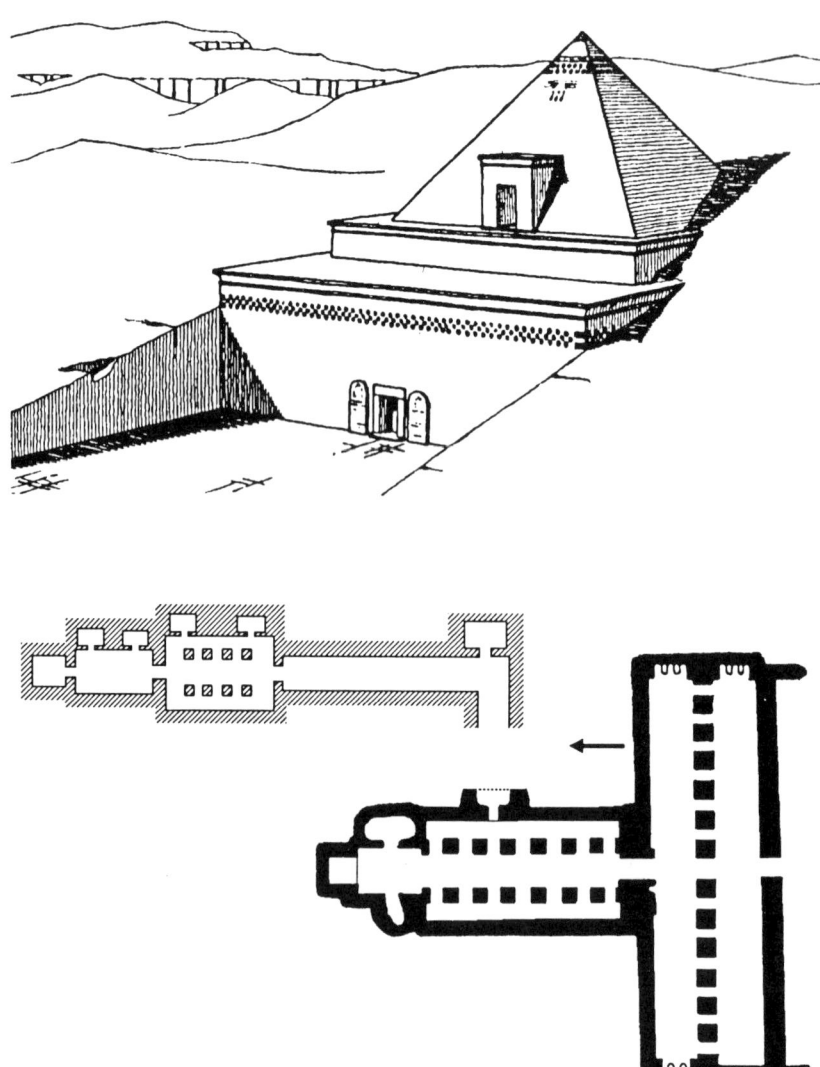

42. Tomb of the high priest of Amun, Nebwenenef, on Dra Abu el-Naga (TT 157, time of Ramesses II): reconstruction and plan. (Reconstruction: Ludwig Borchardt, courtesy of Akademie-Verlag, Berlin.)

Private tombs of the New Kingdom

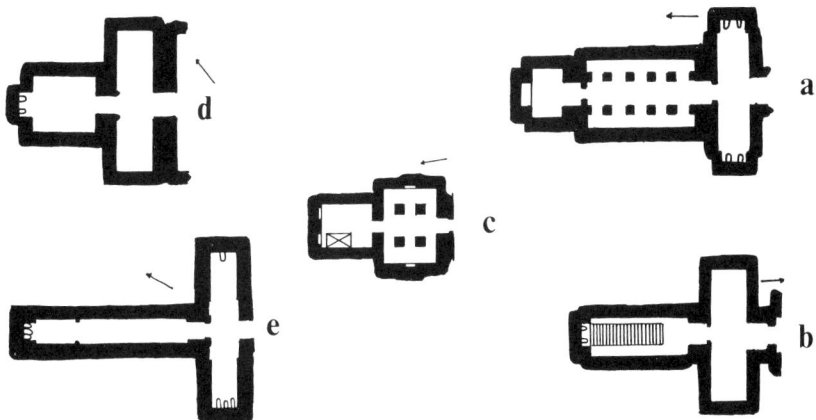

43. Private tomb-chapels of the Ramesside Period: (a) Pennesuttawy (TT 156, Dra Abu el-Naga); (b) Khaemopet (TT 105, Sheikh Abd el-Qurna — both Nineteenth Dynasty); (c) Inhurmose (time of Merneptah — Naga el-Mashayikh); (d) Amunmose (TT 149); (e) Amenemopet (time of Ramesses III-V — TT 148, both Dra Abu el-Naga).

The end of the dynasty

A relatively small number of Theban tomb-chapels can be dated to the last three reigns of the Eighteenth Dynasty; this is probably in part due to the vagaries of preservation, but there are indications that more notables were being buried near Memphis, in the north, where the court spent much of its time. Excavations begun during the 1970s have revealed a number of important tombs at Saqqara belonging to such people as the general (later king) Horemheb and the treasurer Maya. These tombs resembled small free-standing temples (figure 40, b), with elaborate substructures approached by vertical shafts, in at least one case including a burial chamber lined with stone and decorated in relief. Other tombs were cut into the edge of the desert escarpment, such as the burial of the vizier Aperel.

Other tombs cut away from Thebes at around this time include the tomb of Amenhotep (figure 39, c) at the remote site of the Bahriya Oasis, of which its owner was governor; however, most tombs out at the oases are of much later date.

The Ramesside Period

A considerable number of tombs of the earlier Ramesside epoch are now becoming known at Memphis, but a large number lie at Thebes; besides the major tomb-chapels, at Deir el-Medina there are many smaller sepulchres built by the workmen responsible for the construction of the royal tombs of the Biban el-Moluk (figure 44 — see further chapter 7).

One of the most interesting of the major tombs is that of Nebwenenef, high priest of Amun under Ramesses II. On the hillside of Dra Abu el-Naga a pyramid surmounts the rock-cut chapel, whose roof is supported by no fewer than 24 columns; below this is a substructure of considerable size, including an eight-columned hall (figure 42). In addition to these relatively conventional elements on the hill, Nebwenenef also possessed a free-standing chapel almost opposite them in the plain. Very few nobles are known to have had such a monument, one exception being Amenhotep-son-of-Hapu in the time of Amenophis III.

Besides such elaborate complexes, other Ramesside chapels continued to employ the old T-shaped plan (for example, figure 43, b, d, e); some, such as that of the priest Amenemopet, were of considerable size, with a number of group statues and ritual scenes. These supplant the 'daily life' depictions of earlier tombs and are characteristic of Ramesside sepulchres. Agricultural scenes, where they appear, are drastically pruned, while hunting, fowling and similar representations give way to those of adoration and extracts from the various funerary 'books'.

Rock-cut tomb chapels of the period exist at many sites outside the Theban area, random examples including el-Kab, Asyut and Beni Hasan. Interesting tombs are those of Inhurmose at Naga el-Mashayikh, part of the cemetery of the ancient city of This (figure 43, c), and a number in Nubia, particularly those of Penniwt (Aniba) and Nakhtmin (Dehmit).

After the reigns of the last kings Ramesses, rock tombs of the traditional form apparently ceased to be cut at Thebes and are extremely rare elsewhere. Power moved to the flat Delta, where new, built, forms of tomb became current.

5
Royal tombs of the Ramesside era

The Nineteenth Dynasty
After the death of Horemheb, the crown passed to his vizier, Paramesse; as King Ramesses I he is generally regarded as the founder of the first of the two dynasties that are collectively known as the Ramesside Period.

King Ramesses began the construction of a tomb in the Kings' Valley, but little is known of its intended plan, as work was stopped at the bottom of the second stairway by the monarch's premature death. Here, a small rectangular burial chamber was cut and decorated (figure 46, a); when first opened, the tomb still contained his unfinished sarcophagus and other funerary equipment; some of the latter is now in the British Museum.

His son, Seti I, cut his tomb alongside that of his father; its plan (figure 46, b) represents a development of that of Horemheb, while its decoration, in extremely fine bas-relief, extends throughout the length of the tomb for the first time. No trace of a sarcophagus has ever been found in the tomb; the king appears to have been satisfied with a calcite mummiform coffin as the outer container for his nest of wooden and (possibly) golden cases.

Below the burial chamber is a most curious passage, over 136 metres long, without certain parallel in any other tomb. Its end has never been reached, but it appears to be approaching the level of the water table, leading to the suggestion that the passage was intended to link the sepulchre with the life-giving waters of the Nile.

A collapsed wall suggests that a similar passage lies under the burial chamber of Ramesses II, but the whole tomb is so encumbered with debris that this and other detail remain to be confirmed. In its architecture the tomb includes a number of innovations, particularly an increased degree of symmetry about the long axis and the reintroduction of a slide into the centre of the stairways. The other major change is seen with the burial chamber, for its era uniquely situated at right angles to the axis: its design places the vaulted crypt between two rows of columns, a form followed for the remainder of the New Kingdom (figure 46, c). No sarcophagus has ever been identified.

The tomb of Merneptah (figure 46, d) is essentially identical, with a more perfect symmetry. The sepulchral hall (figure 47) once contained no fewer than three nested sarcophagi, and within these a calcite coffin, but only the lids of the outer two remain intact in the tomb; the third sarcophagus was reused at Tanis, while a fragment of the coffin is in the British Museum.

44. Necropolis of the workmen of the royal tombs at Deir el-Medina. As highly skilled masons and artists, the workmen were able to construct finely decorated tombs for themselves and their families on the hillside overlooking their village, many being equipped with pyramids.

45. Central area of the Kings' Valley; at the far left is the tomb of Seti II, with those of Ramesses III and Horemheb in the centre.

Royal tombs of the Ramesside era

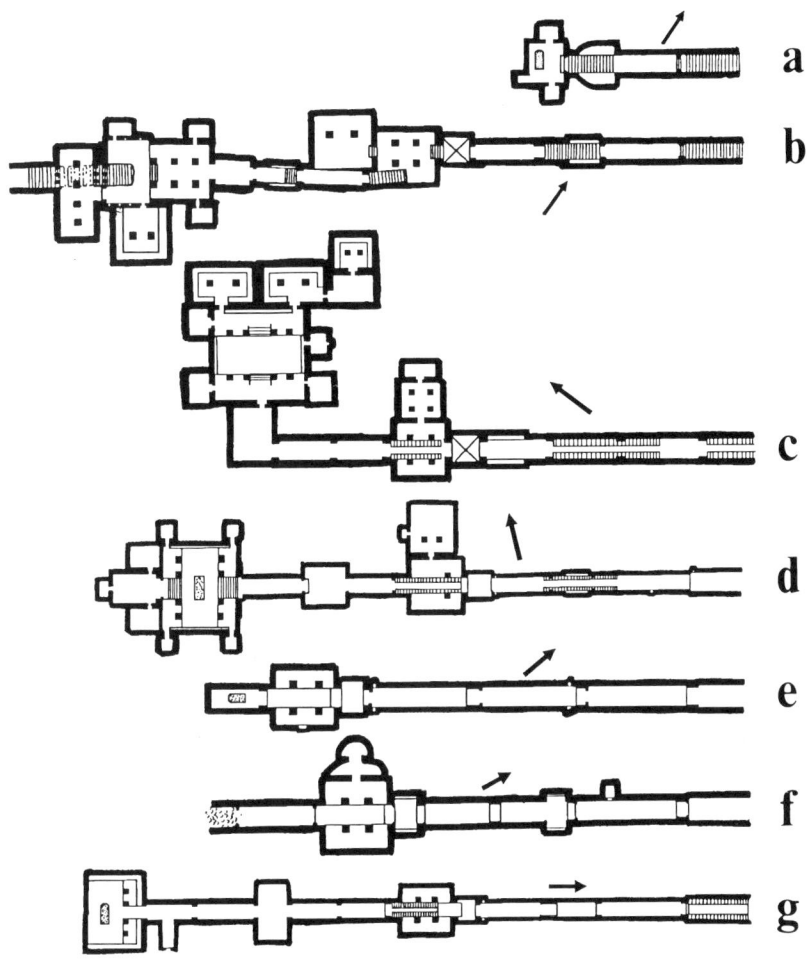

46. Tombs of the kings of the Nineteenth Dynasty. (a) Ramesses I (KV 16); (b) Seti I (KV 17); (c) Ramesses II (KV 7); (d) Merneptah (KV 8); (e) Seti II (KV 15); (f) Amenmesse (KV 10); (g) Siptah (KV 47).

None of the remaining kings of the dynasty appear to have completed the construction of their tombs, although it is clear that all were intended to be essentially of the same design as Merneptah's. It seems likely that the construction of KV 15, the tomb of Seti II (figure 46, e), was interrupted by the temporary unsurpation of the throne by his son (?) Amenmesse; the latter's tomb (figure 46, f) had its decoration erased

47. Burial chamber of Merneptah (KV 8), showing remains of decoration, damaged by flooding, and the lid of the second sarcophagus. (Harry Burton, courtesy of the Griffith Institute, Oxford.)

after Seti's restoration to the throne (figure 48), was later reused and is now largely filled with debris.

The dynasty closed with the reigns of Siptah and Seti II's widow, Tawosret; Siptah's KV 47 (figure 46, g) was only partially decorated and its burial chamber only two-thirds cut, while Tawosret's tomb, modified on her various changes in status, was later usurped for Sethnakhte, the first king of the Twentieth Dynasty.

The Twentieth Dynasty

At the beginning of his reign Sethnakhte began to cut a tomb in the Kings' Valley (KV 11), but it was far from finished on his death, less than two years later. His son, Ramesses III, accordingly took over that of Tawosret (KV 14; figure 49, a), hurriedly modifying its decoration in the seventy days allocated to Sethnakhte's embalming.

Ramesses III then appropriated and completed the unfinished KV 11; this massive sepulchre contains unique paintings of earthly life in the

Royal tombs of the Ramesside era

eight chambers that open off the second corridor, besides an exceptionally complete set of mythological reliefs, and modifies the form of the burial chamber to place the sarcophagus along the axis, rather than across it (figure 49, b). Unfortunately, much of the tomb is now ruinous.

With the exception of the blocked KV 18 of Ramesses X, the form of which remains an enigma, all the remaining Ramesside royal tombs may be seen to be unfinished in some way or other. KV 9 (figures 49, d, and 50), begun by Ramesses V, was essentially completed by his uncle Ramesses VI, but Ramesses IX's was cut short and those of Ramesses IV and VII (figures 49, c, e) redesigned on a reduced scale. The tomb of Ramesses VIII has never been identified.

48. (Above) Left door jamb of the tomb of Amenmesse, with erased, but still readable, texts.

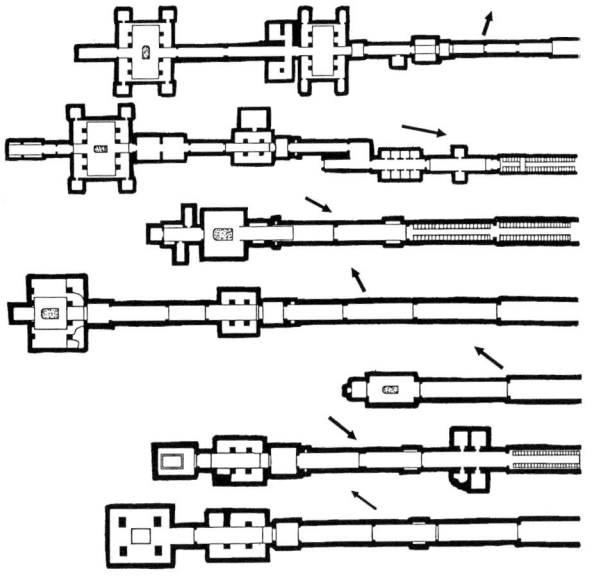

49. (Left) Tombs of the kings of Twentieth Dynasty: (a) Tawosret and Sethnakhte (KV 14); (b) Ramesses III (KV 11); (c) Ramesses IV (KV 2); (d) Ramesses V and VI (KV 9); (e) Ramesses VII (KV 1); (f) Ramesses IX (KV 6); (g) Ramesses XI (KV 4).

50. First corridor of the tomb of Ramesses VI. (Harry Burton, courtesy of the Griffith Institute, Oxford.)

Royal tombs of the Ramesside era

The last tomb to be cut in the Valley of the Kings was that of Ramesses XI (KV 4; figure 49, g), hardly any of the decoration of which was begun; few traces of a primary burial were found when the tomb was cleared by John Romer in the late 1970s. Under Ramesses VII the conventional sarcophagus had been replaced by a huge inverted granite box over a cut in the floor, and now under the last of the line there appeared in the centre of the burial hall a deep shaft, presumably intended to hold one or more coffins.

The tombs of the royal family

In contrast to the scattered burials of the Eighteenth Dynasty, many of the offspring and wives of Ramesside kings found rest in a single wadi in the southern part of the Theban necropolis, now known as the Biban el-Harim (Valley of the Queens). The earliest certain decorated tombs are those of Sitre, wife of Ramesses I (QV 38), and Tuy, wife of Seti I (QV 80), but the best known are of the time of Ramesses II and Ramesses III. Two examples from the former's reign are those of his wife, Nefertari, and daughter Bintanat (figure 51, a, b), Nefertari's being in many ways a miniature version of the grave of her husband.

51. Tombs of members of the Ramesside royal family: (a) Nefertari, wife of Ramesses II (QV 66); (b) Bintanat, daughter of Ramesses II (QV 71); (c) Khaemwaset (QV 44); (d) Unknown (KV 3), both sons of Ramesses III; (e) Tyti, wife of Ramesses X (QV 52).

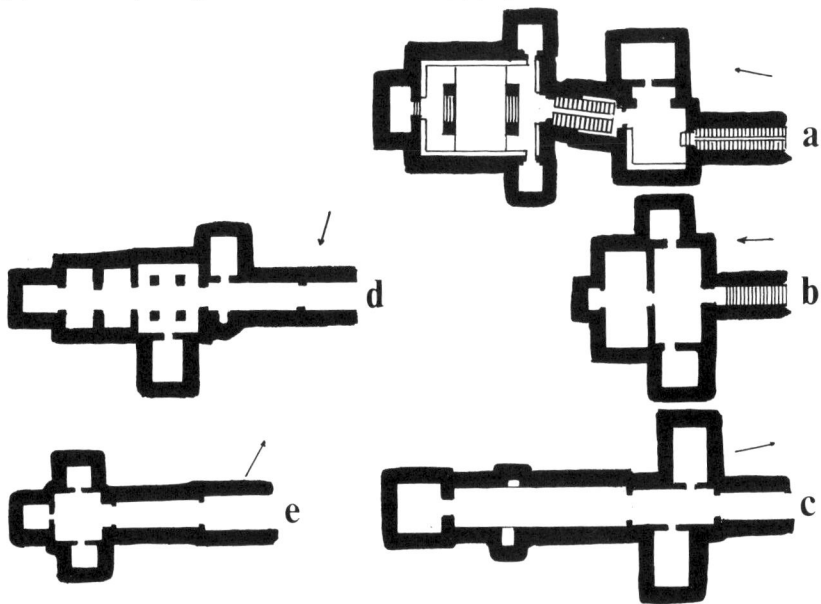

52. Tomb of Mentuhirkopshef, son of Ramesses IX (KV 19); the path on the right leads to that of Tuthmosis IV.

Ramesses III cut a series of tombs for his sons, one large, but almost undecorated, example in the Kings' Valley (figure 51, d) and five in the Biban el-Harim (for example, figure 51, c). The tombs of a number of later Ramesside queens also lie there, but Mentuhirkopshef, son of Ramesses IX, was buried in the Kings' Valley (figure 52), as were the king's wife and mother, in the former tomb of Amenmesse.

6
Later tombs

The Third Intermediate Period

The kings of the period that followed the last Ramessides ruled from the flat Delta, where no cliffs existed to hold the tombs of themselves or their followers. The royal tombs at Tanis, the new capital, were stone-built structures sunk in temple courtyards, as were those of the high priests of Memphis; the style was even found at Thebes, where the tomb of the king/high priest Harsiesis lay in front of the mortuary temple of Ramesses III at Medinet Habu.

A few Theban tomb-chapels were usurped during the period, but in most cases the new, lavishly decorated coffins were laid away in small bare rock-cut chambers, sometimes taken over from earlier owners.

Two larger works are long galleries in the area of Deir el-Bahri which respectively contained caches of royal mummies and those of Twenty-first Dynasty priests.

Another rock-cut tomb in which work was carried out during the Third Intermediate Period was the Serapeum at Saqqara, the complex of galleries begun to contain the mummies of sacred Apis bulls under Ramesses II, and subsequently extended through to the Ptolemaic Period. Before Ramesses II's time the bulls had been laid to rest in individual rock tombs, surmounted by free-standing chapels.

The Late Period

In the Twenty-sixth Dynasty there was something of a renaissance of Egyptian culture and power, and during this period there came to be built the largest rock tombs of any era. The kings were buried at Sais in sepulchres rather similar to those of Tanis, while the high priestesses of Amun were interred in shafts below built chapels at Medinet Habu (figure 53). However, a number of officials built truly monumental tombs at Thebes and Saqqara.

Most Theban examples lay on the Asasif (figure 54), including the biggest of them all, the sepulchre of the priest Pedamenopet (figure 55). A built pylon and forecourt lead to a series of halls and passages, all decorated with ritual and other scenes in bas-relief, in many cases modelled on Old, Middle and New Kingdom prototypes. Deep in the rock lies the burial chamber, just above which is cut a square massif whose form imitates the sarcophagi of the kings from Akhenaten to Horemheb, with the figures of goddesses at its corners.

Other, smaller tombs in the same general area included that of Nesipaqashuti, built in the courtyard to a Middle Kingdom chapel.

53. Chapels of the high priestesses of Amun, Amenirdis I (left) and Nitokris, Shepenwepet II and Mehytenweskhet (right), at Medinet Habu.

54. The Asasif, Western Thebes, with the group of Saite tombs in the centre.

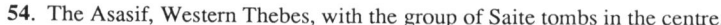

Later tombs 53

As well as tombs similar to the sepulchres of the Asasif (for example, that of Bakenrenef), a group of interesting shaft tombs was built at Saqqara in the period spanned by the (Saite) Twenty-sixth and (Persian) Twenty-seventh Dynasties. Their burial chambers were constructed at the bottom of huge pits, each entered from a small shaft to one side; the chamber had pottery-sealed openings in its roof, which were broken after the burial. This allowed sand to enter from the refilled main pit, allowing the whole tomb to fill with sand in such a manner that digging any out would result in more pouring in, as an effective defence against robbery.

During the Late Period necropoleis are known in many locations, though most rock tombs are of very simple design and infrequently decorated. One may note examples of the more elaborate kind at Fustat, Giza, el-Hiba, Beni Hasan, Koptos and Naga el-Hisaya, as well as at the Bahriya and Siwa oases.

The Ptolemaic and Roman Periods

Rock tombs of standard Egyptian types continued under the Hellenic rulers who followed Alexander the Great, but various forms of built

55. The Saite tomb of Pedamenopet (TT 33) in the Asasif, the largest tomb at Thebes.

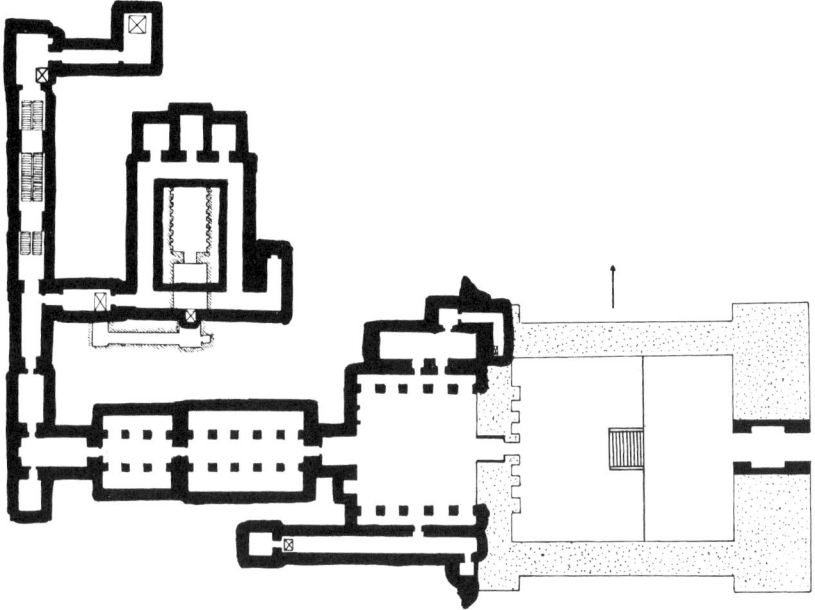

56. The Graeco-Roman necropolis of brick and stone tomb-chapels at Tuna el-Gebel: burial chambers lay at the bottom of shafts below the chapels.

57. A tomb-chapel at Tuna el-Gebel.

Later tombs

tombs in stone and brick were common (figures 56 to 58). As the European domination continued, new forms appeared, of which good examples are to be seen in the catacombs of Kom el-Shuqafa, in Alexandria. Although containing certain Egyptian decorative motifs, their plans are wholly alien and were designed to accommodate bodies whose numbers ran into the hundreds; their discussion lies beyond the scope of the present work.

58. Façade of the tomb of Petosiris at Tuna el-Gebel (*c.* Ptolemy I), closely following the form of a contemporary temple.

7
Design and construction

As with most aspects of Egyptian engineering, monumental sources reveal nothing about the construction of rock-cut tombs. However, documents used by the workmen employed in tomb construction combine with observations of the monuments themselves to allow us to give some account of the procedures involved in the cutting of a rock tomb.

Design

Amongst papyri and ostraca from the Theban necropolis are a number which deal with the design of sepulchres, some noting dimensions, some giving complete or partial plans. The most impressive is a papyrus in Turin which gives the plan of the tomb of Ramesses IV (KV 2), but its purpose remains somewhat uncertain. Other items, particularly the ostraca, are more likely to be working documents, including notations of volumes of stone to be removed, and sketches of certain architectural elements, but it is not clear what form the master plan took.

Regarding the planning of the decoration of a tomb, the recurrence of particular details at widely separated sites suggests that pattern books of motifs existed, although none has survived. In the Saite Period another approach was adopted for certain Theban tombs, parts of whose decoration were directly copied from far more ancient monuments; a particularly impressive example is that of the tomb of Ibi at Thebes, much of whose adornment was based upon that of a namesake at Deir el-Gebrawi, 320 km (200 miles) and 1600 years away.

Construction

Fundamental to construction was the establishment of a centre line; cutting proceeded from the centre out, and from the ceiling down; numerous examples exist of tombs where central axis at roof level is finished, but whose wings are incomplete and rise in steps to the ceiling at the extremities. These steps are the result of the method of quarrying, which removed blocks of limestone in layers; tools used were both stone and metal (copper, later bronze), the latter used for the finer work.

Decoration ideally took place as soon as a wall was freed from the rock matrix; where painted decoration was to be applied, the wall was covered with a layer of mud plaster, finished with finer gypsum, after which the draughtsmen and painters got to work. In this case, the rock-cut wall could be quite rough, particularly if the quality of the stone was poor; however, where relief was to be employed, it had to be brought to a much finer finish, with plaster used to make good faults and other

Design and construction

59. Unfinished tomb 11 at Beni Hasan, showing the manner in which the limestone matrix was removed.

blemishes. In some cases a new piece of stone could be inserted, but in extreme instances a complete stone lining could be employed.

A curious practice seen in the Biban el-Harim was the production of complete tombs, fully decorated, but lacking the owners' names and titles. All these tombs were intended for ladies of the royal family. A similar practice is seen with smaller items of equipment, clearly produced as undertakers' stock, with the gaps to be filled in for the eventual user.

An exception to the above mentioned decorative sequence is to be found in the Biban el-Moluk tombs prior to Horemheb; in these there is evidence that the application of the actual paintings followed the mummy's interment. The walls will have been fully prepared, with ground and border colours painted in, but the images of the gods were applied as part of the ceremonies that transformed the tomb into the eternal resting place for the living god. Such a ritual became impossible, however, once the much slower decorative style of relief was adopted after the Amarna interlude.

The workmen of the tomb

Most of the artisans who laboured to produce the Egyptian art and monuments that continue to excite wonder millennia later remain anonymous; however, a few of their names are known, in particular those of the men who built the Ramesside royal tombs. Their village, Deir el-Medina, has been fully excavated and documents recovered allow us to follow much of the life and work of the community. Contrary to the Hollywood image of slaves, working under the lash and killed at the completion of work to preserve the tombs' secrets, the workmen were skilled craftsmen, passing their calling from father to son, and sufficiently sure of their position to strike on occasion in support of a grievance.

Deir el-Medina was established by either Amenophis I or Tuthmosis I expressly to house those responsible for the construction of the sepulchres on the opposite side of the Theban cliff, in the Biban el-Moluk (figure 60). Here the workmen lived with their families, though they spent their weekday nights in a group of huts on the ridge overlooking the Valley of the Kings (figure 61). These settlements were occupied down to the end of the New Kingdom, with a brief break during which

60. The village of Deir el-Medina, Western Thebes.

61. Workmen's huts on the brow of the hill between Deir el-Medina and the Biban el-Moluk.

the community, or part of it, may have moved to Amarna, and from the village itself come huge quantities of papyri and ostraca which represent its administrative documentation under the Ramessides. Further ostraca have come from the Kings' Valley, and certain other sites, which allow us to reconstruct much of the business of constructing royal and other tombs. Apart from these technical matters, the status and prestige of the skilled workmen become apparent, their skills amply demonstrated by the quality of their work on the kings' tombs and on those that they made for themselves on the cliffs that overlook the village.

Elsewhere at Thebes other groups of specialist tomb craftsmen clearly existed, although far less is known of them, as they did at necropoleis throughout the country; together, they were responsible for the production of remarkable monuments which still delight the eye today, millennia after their authors had passed to 'The West'.

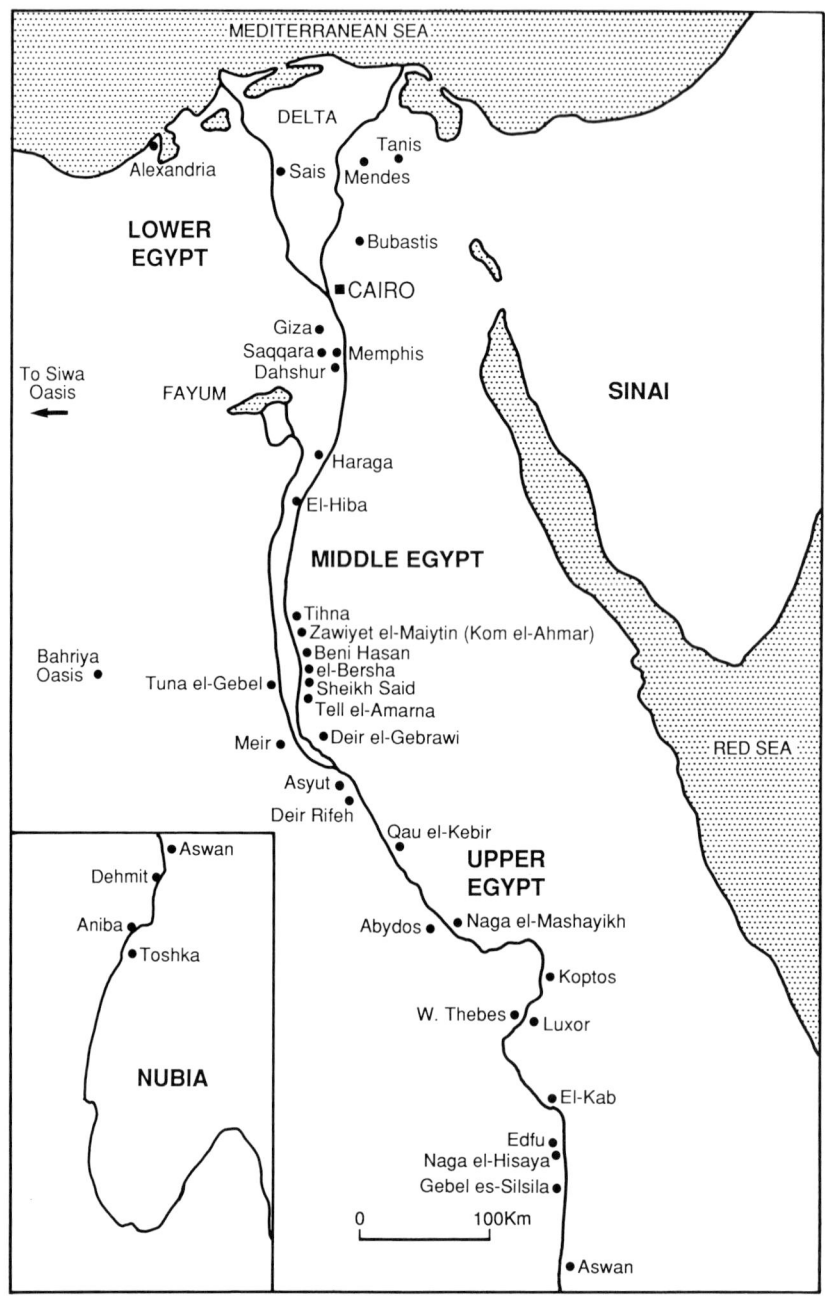

62. Map of Egypt and Nubia, showing the locations of sites mentioned in the text.

8
The future

After millennia of neglect, the rock tombs of Egypt have become part of the world's consciousness during the nineteenth and twentieth centuries. They have been studied and protected from plunderers and, with the dawn of mass tourism, been visited and admired by thousands of people a year. But today they are in deadly danger, from their very popularity and from less immediate manifestations of the modern world.

The survival of the monuments and their decoration has been a direct result of the stable conditions in the arid desert or the hermetically sealed tomb chamber; however, there have been massive changes in their environment in modern times. The most obvious change has been caused by the influx of tourists into the often narrow chambers of the tombs; there is not only the ever present danger of inquisitive fingers, but also the increase in heat and humidity caused by numerous human bodies. Humidity is increasing in many of the more southern tombs from a further source, the creation of Lake Nasser by the erection of the Aswan High Dam, which is also raising the water table in Upper Egypt.

These environmental changes manifest themselves in a number of ways. Most dramatic are movements in the very rock into which the tombs are cut. In some cases this leads to the collapse of pillars and other architectural elements, while far more often the expansion and contraction of the underlying stone causes the cracking, buckling and loss of the painted surface of plastered walls.

Most insidious, however, are the effects of natural salts within the stone and plaster; when stimulated by a change in humidity, crystals grow and push the surface of the stone, with any overlying plaster and pigment, away from the wall, ultimately destroying it.

Two famous tombs which are suffering such damage are those of King Seti I and Queen Nefertari of the Nineteenth Dynasty. Both were affected by flooding soon after their discovery, very severe damage being done to the structure of Seti's burial chamber. The damage in the tomb of Nefertari has been less obvious but just as serious, with large areas of the tomb's superb decoration left in such a fragile condition that it has been closed to visitors for many years.

Since the late 1980s a scheme of work has been undertaken, under the auspices of the Getty Foundation, to conserve the tomb's paintings; a number of techniques have been evolved that will prove of use in other monuments which have suffered similar damage.

However, it is recognised that repairing the tombs will not be enough, and it is proving necessary to close tombs periodically to give them some respite from the rigours of tourist groups. Indeed, some radical schemes see the closure of many tombs to tourists and the construction of replicas as the only way of preventing their destruction; this was the solution adopted to save the cave paintings at Lascaux in France.

While conclusions have yet to be reached, unless urgent steps are taken our generation may see the final destruction of monuments without whose decorated walls and preserved contents our knowledge of the ancient Egyptians and their world would be far poorer.

9
Further reading

Badawy, A. *A History of Egyptian Architecture*. Volume I, Cairo, 1954; volumes II and III, University of California Press, Berkeley, 1966, 1968.

Bierbrier, M. *Tomb Builders of the Pharaohs*. British Museum Publications, 1982.

Carter, H. *The Tomb of Tut.ankh.amen*. Collins, 1923-33.

Dodson, A. M. 'The Tombs of the Kings of the Early Eighteenth Dynasty at Thebes', *Zeitschrift für Ägyptische Sprache und Altertumskunde* 115 (1988), 110-23.

Dodson, A. M. *The Canopic Equipment of the Kings of Egypt*. Kegan Paul International, 1992.

Dorman, P. F. *The Monuments of Senenmut*. Kegan Paul International, 1988.

Hayes, W. C. *Royal Sarcophagi of the XVIII Dynasty*. Princeton University Press, 1935.

Manniche, L. *City of the Dead*. British Museum Publications, 1988.

Martin. G. T. *The Hidden Tombs of Memphis*. Thames and Hudson, 1991.

Reeves, C. N. *Valley of the Kings. The Decline of a Royal Necropolis*. Kegan Paul International, 1990.

Reeves, C. N. (editor). *After Tutankhamun*. Kegan Paul International, 1991.

Romer, J. *Valley of the Kings*. Michael Joseph and Rainbird, 1981.

Smith, W. S. *The Art and Architecture of Ancient Egypt*. Penguin Books, second edition (revised by W. K. Simpson), 1981.

Spencer, A. J. *Death in Ancient Egypt*. Penguin Books, 1982.

Thomas, E. *The Royal Necropoleis of Thebes*. Privately printed, Princeton, 1966.

Ventura, R. *Living in a City of the Dead*. Universitätsverlag, Frieburg/ Vandedhoeck und Ruprecht, 1986.

10
Museums

The following list is a selection of museums possessing significant fragments of the decoration of rock-cut tombs or major items of funerary equipment in their collections. Intending visitors are advised to find out the times of opening before making a special journey.

United Kingdom
British Museum, Great Russell Street, London WC1B 3DG. Telephone: 071-636 1555.
Fitzwilliam Museum, Trumpington Street, Cambridge CB2 1RB. Telephone: 0223 332900.
Sir John Soane's Museum, 13 Lincoln's Inn Fields, London WC2A 3BP. Telephone: 071-405 2107. The calcite coffin and canopic chest from the tomb of Seti I.

Egypt
Egyptian Museum, Midan el-Tahrir, Kasr el-Nil, Cairo.
Luxor Museum of Egyptian Art, Sharia Nahr el-Nil, Luxor.

France
Musée du Louvre, Palais du Louvre, 75003 Paris.

Germany
Ägyptisches Museum, Staatliche Museen, Bodestrasse 1-3, 102 Berlin.
Kestner-Museum, Trammplatz 3, 3000 Hannover 1.

Italy
Museo Archeologico, Via Colonna 96, Florence.
Museo Egizio, Palazzo dell' Accademia delle Scienze, Via Accademia delle Scienze 6, Turin.

Netherlands
Rijksmuseum van Oudheden, Rapenburg 28, 2311 EW, Leiden, Zuid Holland.

United States of America
The Brooklyn Museum, 200 Eastern Parkway, Brooklyn, New York, NY 11238.
Metropolitan Museum of Art, 5th Avenue at 82nd Street, New York, NY 10028.
University Museum, University of Pennsylvania, 33rd and Spruce Streets, Philadelphia, Pennsylvania 19104.

Index

Page numbers in italic refer to illustrations

Abu Hasah el-Bahri, Wadi 28
Abydos 20, *21*, 23, *24*, 33
Ahmose I *21*, 23, *24*
Ahmose-Nefertari 24, *25*, 25
Ahmose-Pennekhbet 34
Ahmose-son-of-Ibana 34
Akhenaten 27, *28*, 30, *36*, 37, *37*, *38*, 51. See also: Amenophis IV
Akhetaten. See: Tell el-Amarna
Alexander the Great 53
Alexandria 55
Amarna, Tell el- 27, *28*, *36*, 37, *37*, *38*, 59
Amduat, Book of 25, 29, 30
Amenemhab *31*
Amenemhat *16*, *17*
Amenemhat II *16*
Amenemhat III 21
Amenemhat-Surero *35*, 37
Amenemopet *41*, 42
Amenhotep *37*, 41
Amenhotep-son-of-Hapu 42
Amenirdis I *52*
Amenmesse 45, *45*, *47*, 50
Amenophis I 23, 24, 58
Amenophis II *24*, 25, *31*, 33
Amenophis III 27, *28*, 30, 31, 35, *35*, *37*, 42
Amenophis IV *36*, 37. See also: Akhenaten
Amunmose *41*
Aniba 34, 42
Aperel 41
Asasif 51, *52*, 53
Aswan 10, *10*, *14*, *16*, 61
Asyut 20, 42
Aten 27, 29, *36*
Ay *28*, 31, *39*, *39*
Bahriya Oasis *37*, 41, 53
Bakenrenef 53
Beni Hasan 11, *15*, *16*, 17, *17*, 20, *20*, 42, 53, 57
Berg el-Hamman *39*
Biban el-Harim. See: Valley of the Queens
Biban el-Moluk. See: Valley of the Kings
Bintanat 49, *49*
Canopic equipment 20, 21, *26*, 30
Chariot *27*, 30
Coffin 14, 43, 49

Dagi *16*
Dahshur 20
Debhen *14*
Dehmit 42
Deir el-Bahri *8*, 14, 23, 24, *25*, *31*, 33, 50
Deir el-Gebrawi 56
Deir el-Medina 41, *44*, 58, *58*, *59*
Deir Rifeh *16*
Dra Abu el-Naga 23, *25*, 33, *40*, *41*, 42
Edfu 34
Fayum 19
Fustat 53
Giza 11, *12*, *13*, *14*, 53
Harsiesis 51
Hatshepsut *8*, 24, *24*, 25, *25*, *31*, 33
Hekaerneheh *35*
Henttawi *34*
Hiba, el- 53
Hierakonpolis 34, *39*
Hor 21
Horemheb *28*, *30*, 31, *31*, *39*, 41, 43, *44*, 51, 57
Hyksos 21, 33, 34
Ibi 56
Inhurmose *41*, 42
Intef II *18*
Kab, el- *31*, 34, 42
Kakherptah *13*
Kamose 23
Ken *32*
Kenamun *31*, 33
Khaefre *8*
Khaemhat *35*
Khaemopet *41*
Khaemwaset *49*
Khenuka *14*
Kheruef *36*, 37
Khety *16*
Khnumhotep 20
Khokha 35, *35*
Khufu *12*
Kings' Valley. See: Valley of the Kings
Kiya 29
Kom el-Shuqafa 55
Koptos 53
Mahu *36*, *38*
Mastaba 11, *12*, 19
Maya 41
Medinet Habu 25, 51, *52*
Mehytenweskhet *52*
Meir 20
Meketaten 29
Meket-Re 17, *19*
Mekhu *14*

Menena *34*
Menkaure *14*
Mentuhirkopshef 50, *50*
Mentuhotep II 11, 14, 17, 23
Mentuhotep III 14, 17, *18*, 19
Mentuhotep IV 19
Merneptah *41*, 43, 45, *45*, 46
Meru-Bebi *14*
Meryetamun 25, *25*
Meryre I *37*
Naga el-Hisaya 53
Naga el-Mashayikh *41*, 42
Nakhtmin 42
Nebwenenef *40*, 42
Neferneferuaten 30
Nefersekheru *37*
Nefertari 49, *49*, 61
Nefertiti 27, *36*
Nekht Ankh *16*
Nesipaqashuti 51
Neterunakht *20*
Nitokris *52*
Nubia 34, 42
Opening of the Mouth 30
Osiris 20, 33, *34*
Paheri *31*, 34
Paramesse 43
Parennefer 37
Pedamenopet 51, *53*
Pennesuttawy *41*
Penniwt 42
Petosiris *55*
Ptolemy I *55*
Pyramid 11, *12*, 14, 19, 20, *21*, 23, 42, *44*
Qarat Hilwah *37*
Qau el-Kebir *16*, 20
Qubbet el-Hawa *10*, 20
Qurn, el- 22
Qurna 25
Ramesses I 43, *45*, 49
Ramesses II *8*, *40*, 42, 43, *45*, 49, *49*, 51
Ramesses III 25, *41*, *44*, 46, 47, 49, 50, 51
Ramesses IV *41*, *47*, 56
Ramesses V *41*, *47*, 47
Ramesses VI *47*, *47*, 48
Ramesses VII 47, *47*, 49
Ramesses VIII 47
Ramesses IX 47, *47*, 50, *50*
Ramesses X *47*, 49
Ramesses XI *47*, 49
Ramose *34*, *35*, 37
Re-Harakhty *36*
Rekhmire *31*

Sabni *14*
Saff 14
Sais 51
Saqqara 11, *15*, *39*, 41, 51, 53
Sarcophagus 20, 21, 26, 29, 30, *31*, 33, 43, *46*, 49
Sarenput II *16*
Senenmut *31*, 33
Serapeum 51
Sesostris I *16*
Sesostris III 11, 20, *21*, 23
Sethnakhte 46, *47*
Seti I 25, *36*, 43, *45*, 49, 61
Seti II *44*, 45, *45*, 46
Sheikh Abd el-Qurna *16*, *18*, *19*, 25, *32*, 33, 34, *34*, *35*, *36*, 41
Sheikh Said *14*
Shepenwepet II *52*
Sheshemnefer IV *12*
Siptah *45*, 46
Siqqat Taqa el-Zeide, Wadi *25*
Sitre *49*
Siwa Oasis 53
Smenkhkare 30
Tanis 43, 51
Tao II 23
Tarif, el- 14, *18*
Tawosret 46, *47*
Tetisheri *21*
This 42
Tihna *14*
Toshka 34
Tuna el-Gebel *54*, *55*
Tutankhamun 27, *29*, 31, *39*, *39*
Tuthmosis I 23, *24*, 25
Tuthmosis II 23, *24*, *24*
Tuthmosis III 24, *24*, 25, *31*, 33
Tuthmosis IV *24*, 26, 27, 27, 35, *35*, *50*
Tutu *37*
Tuy 49
Tyti *49*
Unas 11, *15*
Userhat *36*
Valley of the Kings *22*, 23, *24*, *28*, 30, 31, 42, *44*, 49, 57, 58, *59*
Valley of the Queens 49, 50, 57
Wahki I *16*
West Valley. See: Valley of the Kings
Zawiyet el-Maiytin *37*